Oregon
a photographic journey

photography and text by Greg Vaughn

FARCOUNTRY PRESS

Right: The sandstone bluffs at Cape Kiwanda State Natural Area are among the best places on the Oregon coast for viewing wave action. A hike from the beach at Pacific City, up and over a tall sand dune, leads to this spectacular vista.

Title page: Lupine, balsamroot, and other wildflowers bloom in profusion each May on the slopes and rocky shelves of the Columbia River Gorge. The Nature Conservancy's Tom McCall Preserve at Rowena is among the best places to view the spring show.

Front cover: Perhaps the most recognizable geographic feature of Oregon, majestic Mount Hood towers over the farms, orchards, and forests of Hood River Valley. The orchards of the valley produce many varieties of apples and more than 40 percent of the nation's winter pear crop.

Back cover: The view from Ecola State Park on the northern Oregon coast stretches from Crescent Beach to Haystack Rock at Cannon Beach, and further south to Hug Point. The state park wraps around Tillamook Head and attracts hikers, surfers, beachgoers, and whale watchers. Members of the Lewis and Clark Expedition made their way here in the winter of 1806 to view a beached whale, and when Clark saw the view, he described it as "the grandest and most pleasing prospects which my eyes ever surveyed. . . ."

ISBN: 978-1-56037-660-6

© 2016 by Farcountry Press

Photography © 2016 by Greg Vaughn,
with exception of the "Portland, Oregon" sign™, page 41, © 2016 by City of Portland, used with permission.

For more information about our books, write Farcountry Press, P.O. Box 5630, Helena, MT 59604; call (800) 821-3874; or visit www.farcountrypress.com.

Produced in the United States of America.
Printed in China.

20 19 18 17 16   1 2 3 4 5 6

Above: The iconic 65-foot tall, 6,000-light sign, originally built for the Portland Publix Theatre in 1928, is a city landmark in the downtown Broadway Avenue district. In 1930, the Italian Rococo Revival style theatre became the Paramount Theatre, and in 1984, the historic theatre was renamed the Arlene Schnitzer Concert Hall. Today, "The Schnitz" is the home of the Oregon Symphony and part of the Portland Center for the Performing Arts, serving as a venue for concerts and other entertainment events.

Left: The International Rose Test Garden in Portland's Washington Park has over 8,000 roses representing more than 600 varieties. Other attractions in Washington Park include Hoyt Arboretum, the Japanese Garden, the Oregon Zoo, Wildwood Trail, the Portland Children's Museum, the World Forestry Center Discovery Museum, and the Vietnam Veterans of Oregon Memorial.

Above: A ride in a hot air balloon offers a unique view of northern Willamette Valley farmlands, the Willamette River, and Oregon's famed pinot noir vineyards.

Left: The Oregon State Capitol in Salem is topped with a 22-foot-tall bronze statue titled *Pioneer Man*. Also known as *Gold Man*, the shiny eight-and-a-half ton sculpture by Ulric Ellerhusen is finished with gold leaf.

Above: A western gull rests on the docks at Old Town Bandon. Avid bird watchers can look for over 250 avian species that are regularly spotted on the Oregon Coast Birding Trail. Coastal sea stacks, rocky islets, and headlands are important roosting and breeding grounds for colonies of seabirds.

Right: A couple watches the sunset at Haystack Rock and The Needles on Cannon Beach. At 235 feet, the monolith of Haystack Rock is one of the tallest sea stacks on the Pacific Coast. Hundreds of seabirds nest on the rock each summer.

Above: The Bookmine is housed in the oldest commercial building on Main Street in Cottage Grove. A regular stop on the town's Last Friday Artwalk, the bookstore also sells plants and local handcrafts. The coffee shop at the back retains the original wooden floor from the early days when the building was the Helena Saloon.

Left: Currin Covered Bridge over the Row River is one of the many covered wooden bridges in the Willamette Valley. Also known as the Row River Bridge, this historic span is on the route of the Covered Bridges Scenic Byway in Cottage Grove.

Right: Created by a dam built on the Deschutes River in the early 1900s, Mirror Pond is one of the identifying features of downtown Bend. Several municipal parks flank this portion of the river, including Drake Park, which offers nearly a half mile of riverfront popular for recreation and events.

Below: One of ten beautiful waterfalls on the Trail of Ten Falls in Silver Falls State Park is South Falls, where visitors can walk behind a curtain of water as Silver Creek plunges over a basalt cliff. The park is open year-round and features picnic areas, a campground, and a day-use lodge.

Top left: World famous Powell's City of Books on Burnside Street in downtown Portland covers an entire city block. The bookstore has grown to include five retail locations and an online store with an inventory of over 2 million new and used books. Considered a Portland attraction by many, Powell's hosts many book-related events, including workshops and children's story times.

Bottom left: The Oregon Zoo in Portland's Washington Park houses more than 200 species of animals in five major exhibit areas designed to emulate natural habitats. The 64-acre zoo is actively involved in conservation and endangered species programs, and has been successful in breeding endangered California condors, Asian elephants, and African lions.

Facing page: Salem's Riverfront Carousel, located on the banks of the Willamette River, features more than 40 ornate hand-carved figures. Inspired by old-world style carousels, the attraction is the result of a local citizen's vision and community involvement.

Next pages: Fort Rock, a National Natural Landmark, is the remnant of an extinct volcano called a tuff ring. The name was derived from the towering rock ramparts that rise 325 feet above the sagebrush plains of the eastern Oregon high desert. Once a rich and plentiful marshland, the area was home to some of the earliest known human inhabitants on the continent. Woven sandals made by early Native Americans were found in a nearby cave and are dated at 9,000-13,000 years old, the oldest such artifacts yet discovered.

Above: A photographer captures the view of Cascade peaks from Ray Atkeson Memorial Viewpoint on Sparks Lake. Atkeson was a pioneer in large-format color photography and was named Oregon's Photographer Laureate in 1987. The view of the Three Sisters and Broken Top mountains from Sparks Lake is perhaps his most famous image.

Left: Tumalo Falls in the Deschutes National Forest on the outskirts of Bend is a favorite destination for visitors and residents alike. A short walk leads to the main viewpoint, with a longer trail continuing upstream along Tumalo Creek to additional waterfalls.

An aerial view of Crater Lake National Park after an early winter snowstorm reveals the conical shape of Wizard Island, the only cinder cone to rise above the pure blue waters of the deepest lake in the United States. The volcanic caldera that holds the lake was formed when Mount Mazama, at one time 10,000 to 12,000 feet high, blew its top in a cataclysmic eruption about 7,700 years ago.

Above: A winter snowstorm dusts western hemlock and Douglas-fir trees in Mount Hood National Forest. The dense coniferous forests of the western Cascades are among the most species-diverse natural habitats in the world.

Right: A herd of about a hundred Roosevelt elk live year-round at the Dean Creek Elk Viewing Area along Highway 38 near Reedsport. Named for President Theodore Roosevelt, these are the largest variety of elk in North America.

Facing page: Hells Canyon is North America's deepest river gorge, measuring over a mile deep from the lowest point on its western rim and more than 8,000 feet deep at the eastern rim. Hat Point Overlook east of Joseph provides spectacular views of the Wild and Scenic Snake River far below. Visitors can climb to the top of the fire lookout at Hat Point for an even more expansive vista.

Above: Lan Su Chinese Garden was built by artisans from Portland's sister city of Suzhou and is considered to be the most authentic Chinese garden outside of China. A visit to Lan Su is a beautiful way to experience Chinese culture and the tradition of combining art, architecture, design, and nature.

Left: Portland Japanese Garden in Washington Park is composed of five different garden styles which are influenced by Shinto, Buddhist, and Taoist philosophies. A place of beauty, peace, and harmony year-round, it especially entices seasonal visitors with colorful spring blossoms and autumn leaves.

Above: On a clear day, the west rock shelter built by the Civilian Conservation Corps at the top of Cape Perpetua offers a spectacular view of Oregon's temperate rainforest, more than 70 miles of coastline, and up to 37 miles of open sea. Coastal walkways and the Cape Perpetua Visitor Center just off U.S. Highway 101 are great for whale watching during spring and fall migrations.

Left: Winter storms and high seas bring waves crashing into the eroded sandstone cliffs at Shore Acres State Park. Shore Acres, and adjacent Cape Arago and Sunset Bay State Parks, offer some of the best scenery on the southern Oregon coast, including rocky cliffs, hidden coves, and sandy beaches.

Left: Weatherford Hall on the campus of Oregon State University in Corvallis was built in 1928 and was named in honor of Board of Regents President James T. Weatherford. OSU is the state's leading public research university and one of the only two land, sea, space, and sun grant universities in the U.S.A.

Far left: Buildings on the University of Oregon campus in Eugene include a variety of modern and classical architecture with landscaping worthy of a botanical garden. The academic program at UO focuses on humanities and the arts, social and natural sciences, and the professions.

Below: Willamette University in Salem, founded in 1842, was the first university established in the western states. The private liberal arts university is nationally renowned as a leader in sustainability and civic engagement.

Right: Cabernet sauvignon grapes flourish in vineyards for small wineries like Valley View Winery in the Applegate Valley region of southwestern Oregon. This old vine is likely a descendant of the first wine grape vines in Oregon, which were planted by pioneer photographer Peter Britt.

Far right: The fertile farmland of the Willamette Valley spreads out below rows of grape vines at Champoeg Vineyards. The deep, rich soil of the valley was a strong lure for many of the Oregon Trail pioneers in the 1850s.

Below: Fine pinot noir wine ages in the barrel cave at Archery Summit Winery. The vineyards of the Dundee Hills and surrounding Willamette Valley have gained a reputation for producing outstanding wines of several varieties, most notably the pinots.

Left: A hiker pauses on the Bryce Creek Trail in Umpqua National Forest. Hundreds of miles of trails give access to the verdant forests, lush meadows, and crystal clear creeks of the western Cascades.

Facing page: With over 2 million visitors each year, Multnomah Falls is the most visited recreation site in the Pacific Northwest, and at 620 feet, it is the largest waterfall in Oregon as well as one of the tallest waterfalls in the United States. A trail to the top of the falls includes a walk across Benson Bridge with spectacular, up-close views of the powerful cascade.

Below: Catch-and-release fly-fishing is popular on the North Fork Middle Fork Willamette River. The pristine lakes and crystal clear rivers of the Cascade Mountains are well known for their native and fishery-stocked runs of salmon, steelhead, and several varieties of trout.

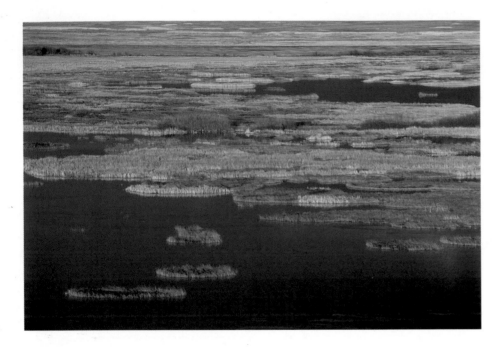

Above: Established by President Theodore Roosevelt in 1908, Malheur National Wildlife Refuge is a critical stop on the Pacific Flyway, offering resting, breeding, and nesting habitat for thousands of migratory birds. The refuge, part of the Great Basin ecosystem, is also home to a large variety of other wildlife. The panoramic view from Buena Vista Overlook spans hundreds of acres of wetlands and sagebrush desert to the slopes of Steens Mountain.

Right: Heceta Head Lighthouse is one of the few remaining coast lights that still casts its beam from a large "first order" Fresnel lens. The classic design and dramatic setting make it one of the most photographed lighthouses in the world. The bare rocks on the point are an important seabird nesting site. A protected cove below the lighthouse welcomes visitors with tide pools and a sandy beach.

Left: *Allow Me*, the iconic bronze statue of a man offering his umbrella by artist J. Seward Johnson, stands at the top of Portland Pioneer Courthouse Square and has been called "the most photographed man in Portland." Located in the heart of Portland, the square is a major tourist attraction, as well as a popular gathering spot and venue for cultural and entertainment events.

Facing page: Newport is known as the Dungeness Crab Capital of the World, and is also home to the beautiful Yaquina Bay Bridge. One of the most recognizable bridges on coastal U.S. Highway 101, it was designed by the visionary engineer Conde B. McCullough. Built in 1934 and listed on the National Register of Historic Places in 2005, the Art Deco-inspired bridge is a testimony to McCullough's principles of building economically, efficiently, and with beauty.

Below: The 125-foot-tall Astoria Column features a hand-painted spiral frieze with scenes depicting events in the early history of the Oregon Territory. Visitors can climb the interior spiral staircase to the observation deck at the top of the column for 360-degree views encompassing the Columbia River, Young's Bay, and the Coast Range mountains.

Right: Viking Soul Food is among the best known of Portland's food carts. Pods of the popular carts, trucks, and trailers are found in the downtown area and in several eastside neighborhood districts.

Below: Shops, art galleries, pubs, and cafés with outdoor seating stretch for several blocks along North Mississippi Avenue. The area has been revitalized and is now one of Portland's most popular neighborhood districts.

Above: The landmark "White Stag" sign has displayed many names throughout the years, originally advertising "White Satin Sugar," to its longest-running version, "White Stag Sportswear," and then to "Made in Oregon." After the city of Portland took ownership in 2010, the lettering changed yet again to the sign seen now that welcomes visitors and workers to Portland's Old Town district. Also known as the "Portland Oregon" sign, this neon-and-incandescent-bulb icon was designated a City of Portland Historic Landmark in 1977.

Left: Forest Park covers 5,157 acres of woodlands on the western hills of Portland and is the largest forested natural area within city limits in the United States. The park's 30-mile long Wildwood Trail is part of an extensive system of pedestrian trails and walkways throughout the city.

Far left: The distinctive glass and steel spires of Portland's Oregon Convention Center rise above the Willamette River and Interstate 5. Pedestrian pathways line both east and west banks of the river through much of downtown Portland. The Willamette starts in the Cascade Range southeast of Eugene and flows 187 miles to its confluence with the Columbia River just north of Portland.

Next pages: Mount Bachelor, near Bend in the Central Cascades, is Oregon's premier winter sports destination and one of the largest ski resorts in the country. The mountain features nearly 3,000 acres of lift-accessible terrain, more than 3,300 feet of vertical, and plenty of quality snow for alpine skiers and snowboarders. The surrounding area offers many miles of trails for cross-country skiing, snowshoeing, and snowmobiling.

Above: Native American pictographs and petroglyphs can be found at several locations in Oregon, especially in the southeast part of the state. These enigmatic figures are etched into the weathered surface of a basalt rock formation overlooking Petroglyph Lake at Hart Mountain National Antelope Refuge.

Right: The view from the summit of Steens Mountain in southeast Oregon encompasses Wildhorse Lake, the Pueblo and Trout Creek Mountains, and the Alvord Desert. Steens, a 30-mile-long fault-block mountain, rises gradually from the sagebrush Great Basin desert to the west, reaching an elevation of 9,733 feet, and then drops abruptly for a vertical mile from its east rim to the Alvord Desert Basin. The unique geology of the mountain includes four huge gorges carved by ice age glaciers.

Next pages: A rainstorm approaches the central Oregon coast at Cape Perpetua. Abundant rainfall nourishes the temperate rainforest in this part of the Oregon Coast Range. Moderate temperatures and up to 100 inches of rain each year in some areas of the coast produce giant Douglas-fir, western hemlock, and Sitka spruce trees.

Above: Classic old wooden barns dot the landscape of the Wallowa Valley in the northeastern corner of Oregon. The Wallowa Valley was the ancestral home to Chief Joseph's band of Nez Perce. A memorial near Wallowa Lake marks the grave of the famous chief's father, Joseph the Elder.

Right: Sunrise bathes a pasture in golden hues in Baker County. Cattle ranching has been an important part of eastern Oregon life and economy since the days of the Oregon Trail pioneers.

Above: Historic Jacksonville in southwestern Oregon got its start soon after gold was discovered at Rich Gulch in 1851. Originally the county seat, the town lost that status to nearby Medford when the railroad bypassed Jacksonville. Most of the town is now officially designated as a National Historic Landmark.

Left: A bronze statue, *Wild Stallion*, by sculptor Lorenzo Ghiglieri stands at the eastern entrance to the town of Sisters in central Oregon. The Sisters Rodeo, held annually on the second weekend of June, was started in 1940. With big purses for a small-town rodeo, cowboys coined the event "The Biggest Little Show in the World." The rodeo continually draws world champion competitors with one of the highest prize purses in the country.

Facing page: Nestled in a valley at the convergence of the Siskiyou and Cascade Mountains, Ashland is the home of Southern Oregon University and the world famous Oregon Shakespeare Festival. Shops, restaurants, and galleries line Main Street and Lithia Plaza. Often referred to as "Ashland's Crown Jewel," Lithia Park offers 93 beautiful acres of gardens, recreation areas, and trails along Ashland Creek. Forty-two acres of Lithia Park are on the National Register of Historic Places.

Above: A short hike on the John Dellenback Dunes Trail near the town of Lakeside leads to the Umpqua Dunes region of Oregon Dunes National Recreation Area. Sand dunes to the north and south are popular with OHV users.

Right: Mount Jefferson is visible through the notch of Asterisk Pass at Smith Rock State Park in central Oregon. Sheer cliffs of tuff and basalt are world renown as a premier location for rock climbing. The park also offers 650 acres to explore with miles of trails for hiking, biking, and horseback riding.

Above: At the summit of McKenzie Pass sits the Dee Wright Observatory built out of lava stone by the Civilian Conservation Corps. The open shelter observatory offers commanding views of the Three Sisters and other Cascade peaks across a landscape of barren lava. The Old McKenzie Pass Highway, open only in summer, follows the route of an 1860 wagon road used by early travelers to cross the Cascades.

Left: The view from the summit of Paulina Peak in Newberry National Volcanic Monument encompasses Paulina Lake, East Lake, and Big Obsidian Flow. In addition to its geological features, the monument is a popular destination for fishing, camping, boating, hiking, and mountain biking. Nearby Lava Lands Visitor Center and Lava Cast Forest offer additional opportunities to learn about this unique environment.

Facing page: The Rogue River flows 215 miles from Crater Lake to the Pacific Ocean at Gold Beach, with 84 miles federally designated as one of the original Wild and Scenic Rivers. A favorite of whitewater enthusiasts, the Rogue is also known for its salmon and steelhead fishing, wildlife viewing, and wilderness hiking on the Rogue River National Recreation Trail.

Above: Hart Mountain National Antelope Refuge in southeast Oregon is home to pronghorn antelope, bighorn sheep, mule deer, redband trout, and a remarkable array of smaller mammals and avian species. The refuge's namesake "antelope" are actually pronghorn, a singular species more closely related to giraffes and okapis. The fastest land animal in North America, pronghorn can attain speeds up to 60 miles per hour, and, even more remarkably, can run at 35 miles per hour for four miles or more.

Right: The John Day River flows through the sage and juniper landscape of central and northern Oregon. Originating in the Strawberry Mountains and winding its way to meet the Columbia River near The Dalles, the John Day is one of the nation's longest free-flowing river systems. Designations as a national Wild and Scenic River and an Oregon Scenic Byway help protect the natural, scenic, and recreational values of the river and surrounding lands.

Next pages: The view of Mount Hood rising above Trillium Lake is one of Oregon's most photographed scenes. The lake is a favorite summer recreation destination, popular for fishing, hiking, canoeing, and family camping. With a summit elevation of 11,250 feet, Mount Hood is the highest point in Oregon. Known to Native Americans of the region as Wy'east, the mountain is a stratovolcano that last erupted in 1865 and is currently dormant.

Above: Bulbs of the common camas were an important food source for Native American tribes of the Pacific Northwest, and fields of the beautiful blue blooms were found in moist meadows throughout the region. Friendly Nez Perce gave the members of Lewis and Clark's Corps of Discovery bread made from roasted camas roots, among other foods.

Left: The North Umpqua River has carved its way through columnar basalt at Toketee Falls, one of the most beautiful and famous waterfalls in Oregon. The two-step drop, totaling 113 feet, is visible from a viewing platform reached by an easy 0.3-mile trail above the river. Toketee, meaning "graceful" in Chinook, is just one of several photogenic waterfalls in the North and South Umpqua watersheds east of Roseburg.

Facing page: The Metolius River springs full force from a basalt cleft in a ponderosa pine forest at the base of Black Butte. One of central Oregon's favorite recreation areas, the valley is known as a great place for fishing, hiking, wildlife viewing, and just plain relaxing. Visitors can choose from several rustic resorts and campgrounds along the river.

Above: Fresh produce stands and U-pick farms are found throughout Hood River Valley. Located between majestic Mount Hood and the Columbia River, the valley's 15,000 acres of orchards are prime producers of apples and pears.

Right: The formal gardens at Shore Acres State Park west of Coos Bay were once part of the grand oceanfront estate of shipping and lumber baron Louis Simpson. The landscaping includes plants and flowers from all over the world, a Japanese-style garden with lily pond, and two rose gardens. The beautiful gardens are a favorite wedding site for south coast Oregonians.

Above: The Historic Columbia River Highway makes a tight loop just below Rowena Crest. When the highway was completed in 1922, it was considered one of the greatest feats of modern engineering. Tagged as the "King of the Roads," the 70-mile route was the first to be named an official U.S. Scenic Byway.

Right: One of two major waterfalls on the McKenzie River, Sahalie Falls plunges 100 feet over a basalt lava cliff. An easy 2.6-mile round-trip hike follows the river through lush old-growth forest to Koosah Falls, another dramatic plunge on the McKenzie.

Above: Designed by the legendary Howard Hughes, the Spruce Goose is the largest airplane ever constructed. Made entirely of wood due to materials restrictions during WWII, the massive plane made only one flight. The Flying Boat, as it is also known, has been restored and is on display at the Evergreen Aviation and Space Museum in McMinnville.

Left: A drive on the Three Capes Scenic Route near Tillamook takes in this view of Netarts Bay on the northern Oregon coast. Netarts Spit, a long stretch of forested sand, separates the seven-mile-long bay from the ocean. Tidal flats here are popular for digging clams, and the bay is a favorite of crab fishermen.

Above: In 1862, five miners on their way to California stopped to camp and discovered gold in a creek near the base of the Elkhorn Mountains in eastern Oregon. The Sumpter Valley Dredge was used to extract gold from the Powder River until 1954 and is now preserved in a state heritage area at the former boomtown of Sumpter. The restored Sumpter Valley Railway offers summer excursions to the historic mining town on a narrow gauge train pulled by a steam locomotive.

Right: The Owyhee River meets Owyhee Lake at Leslie Gulch, a remote canyon in the southeast corner of Oregon. Strikingly reminiscent of Utah's red rock country, Leslie Gulch contains beautiful eroded rock formations of volcanic tuff. The canyon and surrounding uplands are home to rare plants and wildlife such as bighorn sheep, Rocky Mountain elk, mule deer, coyotes, and golden eagles.

Far right: Eagle Cap Wilderness in the Wallowa Mountains is a hiker's and packer's delight with high alpine lakes and meadows, imposing mountain peaks, and glaciated valleys. The Wallowas, unlike the younger volcanic Cascade Mountains, are composed largely of ancient granitic rock. Sunshine Lake, with its view of Eagle Cap peak, is a popular destination for backpackers.

Right: U.S. Highway 101 emerges from the forest and runs along the beach on the southern Oregon coast at Myers Creek near the town of Gold Beach. This section of the Pacific Coast Highway is part of the Cape Sebastian State Scenic Corridor. Viewpoints atop the cape offer panoramic vistas to the north and as far south as Crescent City in California.

Next pages: In 1975, the John Day Fossil Beds in north central Oregon became a National Monument to preserve the unique geological features and ancient fossil treasures of the park's three units: Sheep Rock, Clarno, and Painted Hills. The strikingly beautiful layers of colorful clay at Painted Hills are always stunning but are most breathtaking when viewed in the golden sunlight of late afternoon.

Below: Harbor seals often sun themselves on the rocks just offshore from Strawberry Hill State Wayside south of Yachats. This viewpoint in Neptune State Park along U.S. Highway 101 also offers access to a sandy beach and some excellent tide pools. Resident and migrating gray whales are often spotted along this part of the central coast.

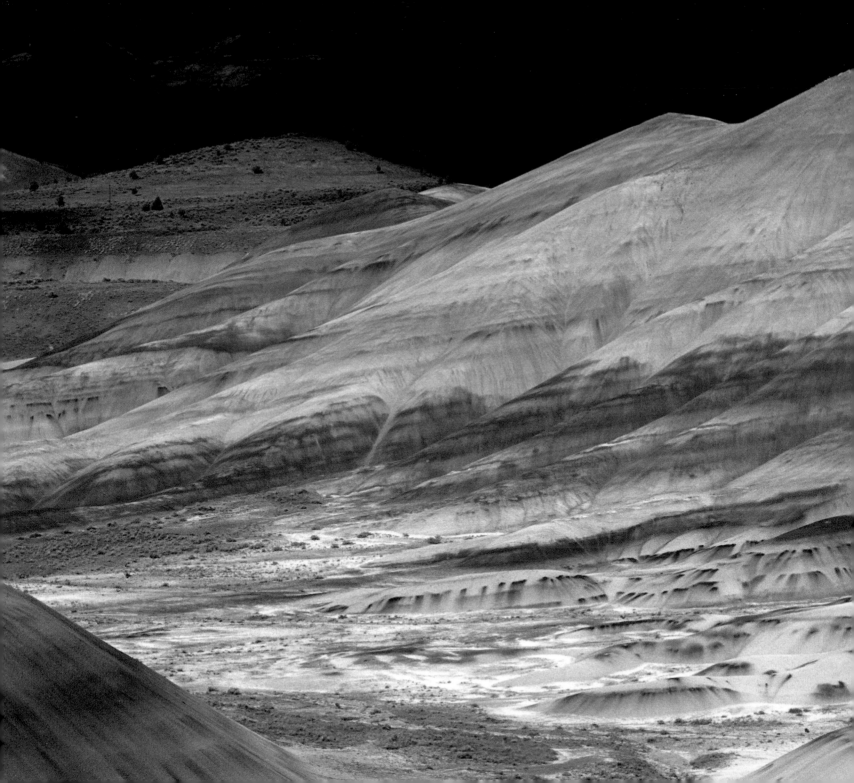

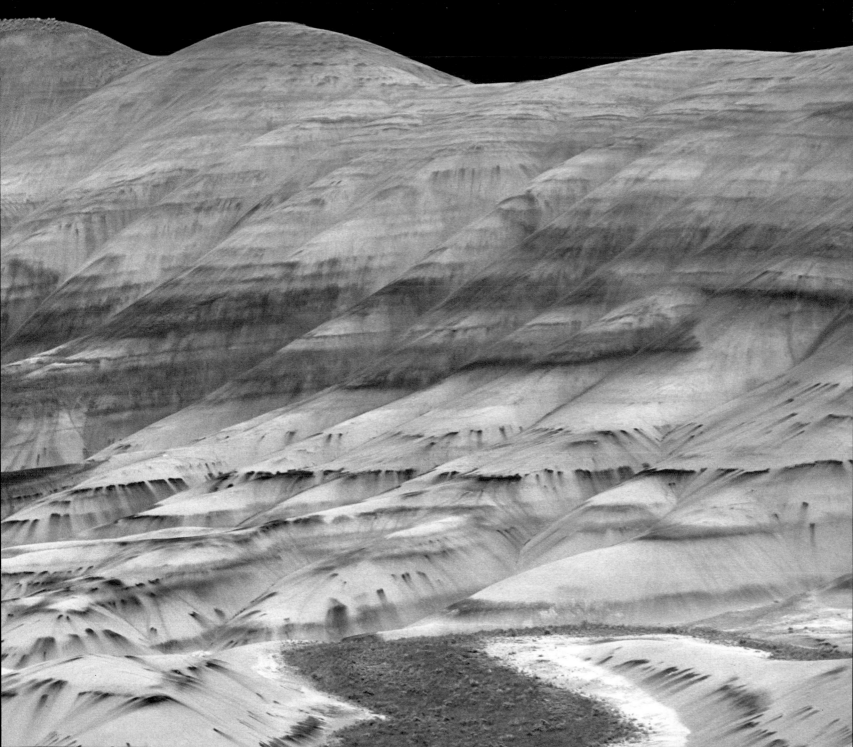

Above: Paintings by Howard S. Sewall on the mezzanine at Timberline Lodge are among the works created as part of the Federal Art Project while the lodge was being built. The highly stylized paintings depict men working with metal and wood, a major part of the lodge's construction.

Top: Timberline Lodge on Mount Hood, a National Historic Landmark, was constructed during the Great Depression of the 1930s as a federal Works Progress Administration project. Timberline Lodge Ski Area is open all 12 months of the year, offering one of the longest ski seasons in North America.

Left: The main lobby at Timberline Lodge features three fireplaces at the base of a 90-foot tall chimney. The lodge was constructed with local stone and timbers, with intricately carved decorative elements placed throughout the building. Among the statistics listed on the bronze plaque on the chimney are Timberline's 6,000-foot elevation and average snow depth of 21 feet.

Above: Between the 1840s and 1880s, hundreds of thousands of pioneers traveled the historic Oregon Trail by covered wagon, on horseback, and afoot in hopes of a better life in the Pacific Northwest. This covered wagon sits on an old stagecoach road at the U.S. Forest Service's Oregon Trail Interpretive Park at Blue Mountain Crossing west of La Grande.

Right: The Corps of Discovery spent the winter of 1805-1806 encamped in a log fort the men constructed near present-day Astoria. Today, visitors can tour a replica of the fort and learn about the Corps' remarkable journey at Fort Clatsop National Memorial, part of Lewis and Clark National Historical Park. Costumed rangers lead interpretive programs daily during summer months.

Above: Proxy Falls drops 226 feet over a lava cliff in two lacy streams. The falls are reached via an easy 1.5-mile loop trail in the Three Sisters Wilderness.

Left: The McKenzie River National Recreation Trail provides an outstanding experience for hikers, mountain bikers, runners, and nature lovers in general. Following the McKenzie River for 26 miles, the trail passes through verdant old-growth forest that is also home to lakes, waterfalls, hot springs, and ancient lava flows.

Next page: The sea stacks at Bandon Beach are a favorite subject for photographers, especially at sunset. Erosion around rocky headlands created these spires of volcanic rock at several locations on the Oregon coast. Some of the monoliths have been tagged with fanciful names like Face Rock, The Mittens, and Wizards Hat.

Oregon resident **GREG VAUGHN** can't imagine a more rewarding occupation than combining photography with his love of travel and nature. For over thirty years he has wandered back roads and backcountry, mountains, valleys, beaches, deserts and islands, capturing images to share the beauty of nature and the wonders of the world.

Greg's photos regularly appear in magazines and websites such as *National Geographic Traveler, VIA, Travel Oregon* and *Alaska Airlines*. He has worked with several calendar and book publishing companies and he is the sole or principal photographer for several books in the Compass American Guides series of travel handbooks. His stock photography is distributed worldwide through agents Getty Images, Alamy, and Corbis.

Greg is a member of the American Society of Media Photographers (ASMP), the North American Nature Photography Association (NANPA), the Society of American Travel Writers (SATW), and the North American Travel Journalists Association (NATJA). His photography has won several awards, and he has received multiple honors from the Society of American Travel Writers and for his guidebooks *Photographing Oregon* and *Photographing Washington*.

To see more of Greg's work, visit www.GregVaughn.com and www.WandersAndWonders.com.